In My World

In My World

Down Syndrome

TIZIANA VAZQUEZ
and
GABRIELLA LLANO

authorHOUSE®

AuthorHouse™
1663 Liberty Drive
Bloomington, IN 47403
www.authorhouse.com
Phone: 1-800-839-8640

Published by AuthorHouse   01/11/2013

ISBN: 978-1-4772-9188-7 (sc)
ISBN: 978-1-4772-9274-7 (hc)
ISBN: 978-1-4772-9187-0 (e)

Library of Congress Control Number: 2012921829

CONTENTS

DEDICATION

This novel is dedicated to our sister and cousin, Dani.
She is our inspiration!

"To the world, you may be one person, but to
one person you may be the world."

—Heather Cortez

MIKA

"Mikaaaa!! Mikaaaa!!"

Screaming. That's what I always hear, people screaming my name, people screaming at me, and people just screaming. I don't like it when people scream; it makes me feel scared.

"Mika, no T.V. Dinner first."

"Mama, please! T.V first, then *papa*."

Mami runs in the room and turns off the T.V.; the screen turns black, and I just see Ariel vanish. I begin to yell and cry and kick, but my mom does not seem to care. She just lifts me up from the floor and drags me to the kitchen. I really don't get why my mom has to be so rough with me. What have I ever done to her? Well, besides the pushing, biting, spitting, and hitting. When I sit down in my chair, my older brother Javi is throwing pieces of *pan* at my little sister Olivia. I stare at my food and just move my fork around the *ropa vieja*. Yuck! I hate *ropa vieja*. I really would rather have some chicken nuggets from McDonalds and a cold glass of chocolate milk.

Papi begins yelling at my siblings and doesn't even notice me covering my ears because of how loud he screams.

"What's wrong, Mika?" Mami asks.

"I want *pollitos* and *choco* milk."

"Mika, eat your food. It's yummy," my father tells me.

I realize that if I don't eat my food, I won't be able to eat dessert, vanilla ice cream. Yum. I am the last one to finish dinner, of course. Mami pours the ice cream into a small pink bowl but still hasn't put it in front of me so I can start eating. I see my mom mix some white powdery stuff and random liquids into the yummy ice cream. I scream out to try and tell Mami to stop.

"Ahhhh, no, no," I say.

My mom ignores me again and keeps mixing the ice cream with that weird stuff. She finally places the ice cream in front of me, but I kind of don't want it now.

"C'mon Mika. Didn't you want ice cream?"

"No! No, ice cream."

My mom just leaves me in the kitchen with the bowl of used-to-be-yummy-ice cream laying in front of me. I eat the ice cream even though it taste like poop, but I finish it, get up from the kitchen table, and walk to the playroom. I turn the T.V. back on, and Ariel flashes back on the screen exactly where I left her.

"Javi get your cleats out of the front door and put them in your room right now!"

"Alright mom, I'll do it later. Calm down."

"No, not later, now."

I always wonder why Javi doesn't just listen to Mami. They are always fighting, and it makes me angry and nervous. Javi is always talking back to Mami and Papi and fighting with Olivia; I can't really fight with them because we have nothing to fight about. Olivia runs into the playroom and sits next to me to watch T.V.

"Hey Mika, want to play?"

"No, T.V now."

"Please Mika, you're always watching T.V."

I push Olivia, but I don't know why. I just got annoyed, I guess. Olivia begins to cry and runs to my mom.

"Mami, Mika pushed me, and it hurt."

"Olivia, I am sure she did not mean it; she just thought you were playing with her."

"Well, I guess she always thinks I'm playing with her when I'm really not."

"I will talk to her. Don't worry."

I hear Mami walking towards the playroom door. She walks in the room and just stares at me. Mami bends down and asks me why I pushed my little sister. All that comes out of my mouth is, "No!"

Mami hates it when I say no. She always tells me the same thing: "Use your words Mika," and this time it was no different.

"Mika, use your words."

"No, no words!"

She looks at me with a sad expression on her face and covers her eyes with her hands. She looks frustrated and tired, so I give her a big hug. Once my arms wrap around her, she opens up and hugs me back. We are hugging for a long time, until Javi walks in and asks Mami to drive him to CVS to get a poster board for a science project he left for the last minute.

"Mom, I need a poster board for my physics project; it's due tomorrow." "Javi, why did you leave this for the last minute?" "I don't know. I just forgot. Please, let's go."

"Fine, c'mon."

Mami looks at me and kisses my forehead. She looks at Javi, "Javi, say goodnight to your sister."

"Mom, we need to go now."

She gives Javi the famous "mom look" that I believe everyone who is a mom has. Javi looks down at the floor and begins to walk toward me. He bends down and gives me a soft hug and kiss on the cheek.

"Goodnight Mika, see ya tomorrow."

Javi and Mami walk out of the playroom and leave me alone to finish my movie before I go to sleep.

I am half asleep when the movie finishes, and Papi walks in to carry me to bed. I do not complain because I am way too tired. Once we enter my room, I am placed on my comfy bed that I absolutely love. Papi pulls out my PJ's and puts them on while I am half laying, half standing. Once my pajamas are on, I crawl into bed, grab Joo-Joo (my teddy bear), and fall dead asleep.

*　　*　　*

"Javi stop it, or I am going to tell on you!"

Javi giggles, "Oh c'mon Olive, it's just Nevil. He won't hurt you."

"Yes, he will. He's a spider! PLEASE STOP."

I hear Javi run into my room and close the door. I sit up and rub my eyes to wake up.

"Javi what happened?" I yawn.

"I'm just bothering Olivia, Mika. You can go back to bed."

"Why are you in my room?"

"I'm waiting for Olivia to come by and check if I'm here, to scare her."

I shake my head and lie back down to try and sleep again. After a long time of trying to force myself to sleep, I decide to get up. I walk into the kitchen and sit next to Olivia.

"Hey sweetie, you slept for a long time," Mami tells me.

"Yes, I was tired."

She gets up and pours herself another cup of this hot black stuff that her and Papi drink every morning. Olivia is eating her favorite cereal, Froot Loops, with a glass of orange juice. Javi is making a huge mess cooking pancakes. Mami puts in front of me a hot bowl of this "oatmeal" I have been eating all my life. This "oatmeal" doesn't even taste like good oatmeal. The "oatmeal" is at first real yummy oatmeal, but then Mami mixes it with a bunch of my gross medicines and vitamins that give the oatmeal the most disgusting taste ever. The bowl of "oatmeal" is laying in front of me all nasty-looking, but I am hungry so I just eat it despite that gaging feeling I get in my throat.

"Mika, don't you like your oatmeal?"

"No! Not good."

My mom just tells me to keep eating so we can go to mass at noon. Every Sunday at noon, my whole family and I go to mass. I like going to mass because everyone is always happy there. Mami and Papi are always smiling, and Javi and Olivia do not fight. I remember that Mami told me Jesus is an accepting and good person; she said He loves everyone equally and is always forgiving. Everyone stands up for Communion, and I follow Papi. Olivia runs past me to catch up to Mami so she won't be last. Everyone takes Communion, and now it's my turn. The priest hesitates to lay the Eucharist in my palms, but my mom nods at him, and he finally places it in the middle of my left hand. I say "Amen" and make the sign of the cross facing the giant crucifix that is up by the altar. When I get back to my seat, everyone is kneeling with their eyes closed and heads on their folded hands. I follow and do the same thing, while

Olivia is lying down across the pew coloring on a piece of paper and eating a bag of goldfish. When we are done praying, everyone sits down and listens to the priest and what he is saying. As the priest walks down the center aisle, he passes by where I am standing on the edge of the pew, lightly touches my hand, and smiles. I don't know why he smiled at me, but I smile back in his direction.

Back at home after dinner, Mami tells me it's time for bed. She puts me to sleep and tells me to get rest because I have school tomorrow.

AVA

"Have a nice day at work, honey."

"Thanks, Hon, love you."

David kisses me on the head and shuts the door behind him on the way out. The clock on the kitchen microwave reads 7:02. Time to wake the kids up. I go down the hallway and knock on Olivia's door. Javi's room is next to Olivia's, so I knocked on his next. The door closest to my bedroom belongs to Mika. I quietly enter her room and find her sitting up in her bed, staring out into space.

"Good morning sweetie, time for school," I say.

"Hi Mami, no school today!" she replies aggressively.

I expected her to not want to go to school, for she never does. But we both know she has to.

"C'mon, Mika. We've got to go to school today. Get up."

She refuses to move, so I carry her out of bed and down the hall to the kitchen. On my way there, Mika shouts,

"Javi! Olivia! Wake up!" which is her usual routine every morning since she is always the first one up.

Right away, Olivia opens her bedroom door with a smile on her face, excited to go to school—well, mostly to see Mika—and heads over to the kitchen.

"Hey, Mika! Good morning!"

"Good morning Olivia, love you!" Mika tells Olivia, with a smile on her face. I sit Mika down on her chair at the table, and Olivia instantly sits next to her.

"Olivia, would you please set the table? Javi seems to still be asleep. *And if he's not awake before I get there,* there'll be no football for the rest of the week," I say a bit too loud, hoping my son heard me.

"I'm up, I'm up, Mami!" Javi shouts from inside his bedroom. Moments later, he joins us at the table.

"Javi!" shouts Mika as soon as Javi comes to her sight.

"Why hello there, little Mika," he replies, giving her a kiss on the cheek. "What's for breakfast, Mami?" he asks me.

"Very funny, Javi. Your cereal is in the cupboard. I put your bowl on the table along with your cup of coffee that Papi prepared for you before he left to work."

"Okay, thanks. And is Mika's food all ready?"

"Almost," I say, forgetting her milk is still warming. I rush over to the milk and turn off the switch, realizing how hot it is. "Shoot", I murmur under my breath. Mika, of course, hears me.

"Okay, Mami?" she asks curiously.

"I'm fine, Mika, don't worry. Here's your baby cereal! Look how yummy," I reply, setting the oatmeal on the table.

"I want to help, Mami! Let me put in the medicines!" Olivia pleads.

"Alright, alright. Just hurry, or else you'll be late for school," I say.

Olivia hurriedly pours in the vitamins and antibiotics that Mika needs daily with her 'baby cereal' (Gerber oatmeal). Mika looks disturbed by the fact that she has to eat this every morning, but she never complains. When

Olivia finishes preparing Mika's breakfast, she finishes her own. I sit on Mika's other side and begin to feed her. The clock reads 7:18.

"Javi and Olivia, look at the time! It's late! Go brush your teeth and get dressed as fast as possible!" I shout.

They obey and rush over to their rooms. I quickly finish feeding Mika, and I take her to her room to dress her as well.

"Okay Mika, let's put on your purple shorts today," I suggest.

"Yay!" Mika accepts.

I put the shorts on her and throw over a white V-neck. We walk to my bathroom and brush our teeth, looking at each other through the mirror, smiling. I brush her hair and run to the front door.

"Olivia, you're ready, right?" I taunt.

"Yep! I'll be right out," Olivia responds.

I let her dress herself today because we were in such a hurry, which I regret. She's only four, so I can't imagine what she put on. Sure enough, she walks out of her room with Javi's old overalls with a yellow t-shirt underneath and her Converse. Her hair is not brushed, and hopefully her teeth are.

"Oh, Olivia, you dressed yourself today! You look beautiful! I'm so proud of you! Did you brush your teeth?"

"Uh-huh, all by myself! I just need you to brush my hair," she says, full of pride.

"Alright, everyone in the car. Javi, you better leave now, too. Your keys are on the table," I say.

"I'm right behind you, Mami! Bye Mika! Bye Olivia! Love you two!" he yells from the hall as he slams his door.

I exit the house and grab the girls' book bags on our way out.

I buckle up Mika in the car, and she grumbles to herself, angry that she has school today. Olivia buckles up beside her and begins to sing her all of her favorite songs. I jump into the front seat and drive off, watching as

15

Javi leaves the house and goes into his car. The clock in the car reads 7:31. School is about ten minutes away, so I think we'll be fine—if I drive over the speed limit, that is. I drop off Olivia first because her school starts early, at 7:45. I give her the book bag and pull her hair back into a ponytail. Mika rolls down her window to wave goodbye. Now, I have to drop Mika off. Her school doesn't start until 8:00, like Javi.

"Mami, music," Mika tells me.

"Okay, Mika. Do you want it loud or soft?" I ask.

"Loud!" Mika replies, giggling.

I play her favorite CD loudly, and she dances along to the rhythm. We arrive to her school shortly after, and Mika realizes it. She begins to squirm, and she begs to stay in the car. I pull her out of the car and carry her to the classroom. I wave to Brooke, Mika's best friend, on the way. I give her to Ms. Owens, and I return to my car before Mika notices I'm gone.

*   *   *

Mika is my world. When David and I found out we were going to have her, we were afraid. We were afraid of who she would be and who she would become. We thought we couldn't raise her and that this couldn't be happening. I remember crying so much that day in my car as we left the doctor. David was trying to comfort me, but he was hurting too. Javi, my older son, had been the perfect child, born with no flaws. I loved him with all my heart and so did David. We wanted another child, and when we got what we wanted, we did not hear what we wanted.

The doctor told us that our daughter had been diagnosed with Down syndrome. Neither my husband nor I had any experience with or knowledge of this disability. The doctor asked if I wanted to go through with this pregnancy, and I said yes. Then, I began to sob. I didn't know it then, but I had said yes to a miracle. Having Mika in my life has been such a blessing, and I have prayed so hard for my family to grow through her, because she is our angel. She may be so different on the outside, but I know how special and beautiful she really is on the inside. She may not do things at the pace of everyone else her age, but she'll get there, in her own time. I choose not to put the *dis* in front of her ability, and neither does she. She's an exceptional little girl, and it doesn't take much to realize it. I love her more than anything.

Having Mika here as a part of the family and as my child is tough and challenging, but rewarding at the same time. To get her to do anything is so difficult, but once she does it, it means so much. Living with Mika is like having a toddler for a *very* long time. We have to do everything for her from taking her to the bathroom, to getting her in and out of the car. It may be a hard job to take on, and she may not be the easiest child to handle. But when she flashes you that huge smile, it's worth all the effort and hard work.

I remember clearly teaching Mika how to crawl. We had a wooden ramp we bought online, and we put it in our hallway. I would sit Mika at the top of the ramp and Javi next to her, and he would cheer her on to prompt her to crawl down the ramp with him. I would get frustrated because all Mika would do was whine and cry. She would scream for what seemed like hours on end because she did not want to learn to crawl. I was dying for her to crawl already; at eighteen months, she was too old not to.

One Saturday morning, I remember I woke her up extra early just so we could spend the entire day learning to crawl. I sat her on the top of the ramp, and I went through the motions with her. Mika, of course, began to cry, and I was so frustrated that I left and told David to take over. He was nervous because he said I was fuming. I went out shopping to clear my head, and when I came back, Mika crawled over to me. I was so happy that I picked Mika up and hugged her tightly. I started to cry. Mika was finally crawling! And she did it without me, which kind of made me sad because I was so sure I'd be the one to get her to crawl. I kissed my husband and thanked him. I remember smiling the rest of the day.

* * *

I run some errands around town until it's time to pick up Olivia from school. We go out for ice cream before getting to the house. When we get home, I unload the groceries and wait for Javi to get home with Mika. When they do arrive, Mika runs inside. I follow her to her room and ask her why she looks so sad.

"What happened at school today, Mika?" I ask her, wondering what could be the matter.

"Brooke," she tells me, in between sobs.

"What about Brooke, Mika?"

"Brooke no play with me."

"Why won't she play with you?" I ask.

"Brooke mean. Off bracelet."

"You took off your friendship bracelet? It's okay, Mika. Tomorrow, Brooke will be nice again," I tell her, hoping it's the truth.

* * *

Today at lunch with David, I get a call on my cell phone.

"Who was that?" David asks, "You don't seem to be too happy."

"It was Mika's school. They want us to meet with the principal in regards to Mika's behavior."

JAVI

I was seven years old when Mika was born and was so excited. I really wanted a little sibling, boy or girl, so I can play with or just bother from time to time. When Mika finally came home from spending two weeks in the hospital, I ran up to her crib and just watched her sleep. She looked different than all the other babies I had seen and was a lot smaller too. I asked my mom why Mika looked different, and she just said that God made her extra special and that not everyone has to look "regular".

When I was 10 years old, I started to notice how diffcrent Mika was compared to all the other three year olds already walking and talking. Mika was still wearing a diaper and sitting in a stroller everywhere we went. I just didn't get it.

One night, my family and I went out to dinner for my dad's birthday. When we arrived at the restaurant, Mika was fine and not complaining, but once we sat at the table and the waiter came to take our orders, Mika just lost it. She started to cry and scream, and everyone started to stare at us. My parents tried to calm her down, but nothing worked. Mika just kept forming a show. I was so embarrassed. The entire restaurant was staring at my family, and even the workers were hovering over our table just watching. My parents finally calmed Mika down, but we had to leave the restaurant to do so. I never really knew why Mika acted up at the restaurant or what caused her to become so aggravated. I had never seen any other child act that way, only Mika.

Finally, I got the courage to ask my mom a question that I knew would cause me to think, "What is wrong with Mika?". Once that question came out of my mouth, my mom began to tear up and hug me. She told me that Mika had something called Down syndrome, and kids that are born with this particular disability look and act differently than normal kids. She also told me that no matter how different anybody is either physically or emotionally, I should always treat them how I would want to be treated, with love and respect. One thing my mother told me that will always be with me is that judging a person does not define who they are, it defines who you are. After the day that I found out Mika had Down syndrome, I became more protective and caring towards her than I would ever be with anyone else.

When Olivia was born two years later, everyone was so happy for my family and especially for my mom. Mika wasn't too pleased with the whole new baby dilemma, and everyone awing and laughing at whatever she did no matter how dumb. I could tell Mika was jealous, but my mom couldn't. She was too happy with Olivia and even happier that Mika had a baby sister to play with. I remember Mami trying to get Mika to at least kiss the baby goodnight, but Mika would just turn the other way and ignore the baby all together. One night, my mom told me to talk to Mika and explain to her how wonderful it is to have a younger sibling and a bunch of other ooie-gooie mom talk. I walked into Mika's room, sat on her bed, and waited for her to just sit down next to me.

"Hey Mika, guess what?"

She just ignored me and kept playing with the doll her best friend Brooke gave her.

"Mika, I know you have been feeling jealous about the new baby in the family, and you feel Mami and Papi won't pay attention to you anymore, but that's not true."

Mika looked up at me and smirked a bit.

"They will always love you and pay attention to you no matter what happens and so will Olivia. I mean you are her older sister," I nudge Mika's shoulder, and we both start laughing.

"Mika, you'll grow to love Olivia, and she will look up to you always. But remember you and me will always be partners in crime no matter what."

Mika looked up at me and smiled. I gave her a huge hug, and we both walked over to see Olivia.

Flash forward four years, and I'm sixteen, a junior in high school and a starter on the varsity football team. Everyone in school thinks I have it all—the looks, the popularity, and the life. I have been pretty lucky. I mean I play the sport I love, and I have two parents who love me and sisters that I adore. Even though everyone thinks I have it all put together, my world was greatly impacted by Mika in ways that no one can ever realize. She has changed the way I view people and treat them; she has helped me see through her eyes that everyone in this world is good and innocent.

I leave to school at 7:30, and my mom reminds me that I have to pick Mika up from school today because she is going to be running errands. I just nod my head and walk out the door biting into the banana that I grabbed before leaving. I pick up my friend Ryan before heading to school. Ryan and I have been friends since middle school. We were in the same homeroom in sixth grade and both played on the same football team.

"Hey man, thanks for picking me up this morning. My car was acting up again, so it's in the shop."

"It's fine dude. I pass by your house anyway."

I pull into the school parking lot and nudge Ryan to wake up from his "five minute power nap," as he so calls it.

"I'm up. I'm up."

I walk into school with the same attitude as everyone else: tired, annoyed, and just not really wanting to be here. Well, I mean it is Monday. My first two classes feel like eternity. Then, lunch comes around, and life just gets so much better. At lunch, Ryan and I sit at a table where these two other guys are studying for some test. The football players all sit together everyday. It's kind of annoying. They're like a cult. Frank, the head quarterback and oldest one on the team, walks past me and just gives me a face that makes him look like some animal stalking its prey. Ryan bumps my shoulder.

"Hey Jav. Look. There's big Frank."

"Yeah, I know. What's his problem?"

"Who knows? But you're definitely part of it."

I look back at Frank, and we make eye contact for a split second. But then Frank's girlfriend Lindsay sits beside him, so he turns towards her.

"What have I done to him? I've never even had a full blown conversation with the guy."

"I guess he just hates you because you're a starter on the team and only a junior."

"I guess. Whatever. That's his problem."

After lunch, the rest of my classes go by pretty fast, except Pre-Calculus. That class is just plain torture. Ryan's mom picks him up from school, so I head out to pick up Mika.

When I get to Mika's school, I see Mika and her friend Brooke standing in front of each other and arguing. I get off the car and call Mika over. She just screams out, "No!"

"Mika, let's go! We have to go home."

Mika ignores me and keeps a straight face towards Brooke. A group of girls walk up behind Brooke and ask if she is coming over to play. Brooke nods her head and reminds Mika she can't come. Mika doesn't move; she just rips off the bracelet that she was wearing and throws it at Brooke's face. Brooke covers her face and begins to cry. She tells Mika one last thing, but I couldn't understand what she said. Mika runs up to me and starts sobbing into my chest.

"Home, Javi."

I bend down to be face to face with her, "What happened Mika?"

"Brooke was being mean to me."

I don't ask any more questions because I can see how terrible Mika is feeling. The car ride home is dead silent; Mika doesn't want to talk so she just looks out the window. I pull into the driveway and find my mom gardening in the front yard. Mika gets out of the car and runs into the house.

"Mika what's wrong?" asks my mom.

"Forget it mom. She won't talk to anyone."

"Javi, what happened with Mika?"

I walk over to my mom, "I don't really know. When I picked her up from school, I saw her fighting with Brooke, but she wouldn't tell me what it was about."

"Are you sure it was Brooke she was fighting with?"

"Yeah, I'm positive."

My mom picks up her gardening tools and walks in the house to go check on Mika. I hear Mika crying in her room, and my mom comforting her so she feels better. I go to the kitchen to get something to eat and see Olivia sitting in front of the cookie jar gobbling down all the cookies she can before mom sees her.

"Boo!"

Olivia turns around, "AHH! Javi, you scared me."

"What are you doing?" I say laughing.

"I'm just having a snack."

"A snack? It looks like your having a full out cookie feast."

Olivia gets down from the chair and turns toward me, "Do you think Mami will know I ate all the cookies?"

I can't help but laugh at Olivia. Her mouth and hands are covered in chocolate, and her shirt is full of crumbs. "She will if you don't get clean."

Olivia runs off to the bathroom to get cleaned up before anyone else sees her. I make myself a sandwich and sit down to watch some T.V before I start homework. A couple of minutes after I start to eat, I hear Mika walk out of her room and go into the playroom. My mom walks in the kitchen and sits in front of me, "Alright, I think she will be ok."

"What happened?"

"She just told me that Brooke won't play with her."

"Oh, that's why she ripped off her bracelet."

"Yeah and what was that all about?"

I take a bite of my sandwich before I start talking, "I don't know the whole story I just saw Brooke scream at Mika, and then Mika ripped her bracelet off and threw it at Brooke.

My mom looks surprised; "She threw the bracelet at Brooke?"

"Yeah."

"How was Brooke?"

"She started crying a little."

"Oh God."

My mom gets up and walks out of the kitchen; I finish eating and go to my room and start with my homework.

MIKA

It's really cold where I am. The ground is covered with freezing white powder, and the trees have no leaves. No one is around; I am alone and don't know what to do. I feel a sudden heat on my face so I look up and see the sun beaming down on me and everything around me. A second after, I feel the heat go away, and it gets cold again. I look up at the sky and notice that the sun has disappeared. I start chasing the sun and try to find it, but I don't know where it went. The sun makes me happy and feels good on my skin. I want to find it. I want to find it.

I feel someone tugging my arm. I open my eyes and see Mami staring down at me. Mami has always been there for me. She just doesn't understand what it's like to be me, and she never will. She always tells me that everything will be okay, and I try real hard to believe her, but most of the time it just isn't. Mami talks to Javi and Olivia differently than the way she talks to me. Mami acts rougher with me when I act up, but the only reason I act up is because I just want to be treated the same. She tells me I'm special; sometimes I don't see what is so special about a girl like me. I can't talk in full sentences; I don't know how to express the way I feel, and I always get weird stares from strangers. But Mami knows me better than anyone else on the planet. I know how much she loves me, but I don't like it when she gets mad at me. She just doesn't know how I feel. I feel like I have a little person in my mind that is trying so hard to get out but can't.

She tells me I have to get ready for school. I start to think about my dream and how it made me feel. Dreaming to me is an escape from the real world and how hard reality can be. When I dream, there is no screaming, no fighting, and no limits. This particular dream made me happy, but then I got sad because I felt alone and scared.

Mami comes back and carries me out of bed and takes me to the kitchen to eat breakfast.

"Javi! Olivia! Wake up," I shout to wake my brother and sister.

I sit down at the kitchen table and wait for Mami to make my cereal. Olivia helps by putting in all the disgusting stuff, and while she and Javi begin to get dressed, Mami feeds me. She then dresses me, and we're off to school.

When we get there, I don't want to get off the car, but Mami carries me to my classroom anyway. Ms. Owens takes me from her, and we enter the class together. I sit next to my best friend Brooke, but she ignores me and starts talking to Haley. Haley is a girl that has never talked to me and always laughs at me. I have tried to be nice to her, but she doesn't seem to care. Ms. Owens stands in the front of the class and starts the day by reading us a story. I hear Brooke and Haley laughing behind me, and when I turn around to face them, their giggles stop. I notice Haley's finger stop pointing in my direction as soon as she sees me looking at her.

"Mika, turn around," Ms. Owens tells me.

Later, at lunch, I grab Brooke's lunchbox and mine and sit at one of the picnic tables.

"Brooke, here lunch."

Brooke looks mad and runs in my direction, "Give me my lunchbox, Mika!"

I don't know what to do, so I just keep holding on to it. Brooke comes and rips the lunchbox out of my hand and walks away to eat with Haley. I'm not really friends with anybody else, so I just eat by myself.

The rest of the day goes by fast. After school, I go up to Brooke and try to talk to her, but she walks away.

"Brooke! Want to come to my house?"

Brooke ignores me and keeps walking with Haley and other girls. I run to catch up to them, but they turn around just before I was going to tap Brooke on the shoulder.

"What's your problem freak?" Haley said to me.

Brooke seems nervous and looks down at the ground.

"Brooke, want to play?"

"No Mika, she doesn't. She is coming to *my* house."

Brooke turns around and tells Haley that she wants to talk to me alone. Haley and the two other girls walk away and leave me and Brooke alone.

"Look Mika, I am going over Haley's house."

"Brooke, you said you were going to come to my house."

"Yeah, but when I go to your house, it's boring, and all we do is play with baby toys or watch baby movies."

I look at Brooke and ask her one more time if she wants to come over. Haley is now standing behind Brooke and asks if she is finally going. Brooke nods her head and reminds me I am not invited.

"Grow up Mika! We can't be friends anymore. You're still a baby, and I'm not."

I feel tears roll down my cheek, and my throat gets all puffy. I hear Javi from a distance call my name to go home, but I just shout back "No!" Brooke keeps staring at me to see what I will do next. I look at my wrist and see my friendship bracelet Brooke and I made last year. I rip the bracelet off, and full of anger, I throw it at Brooke. She covers her face right after the bracelet hit her and begins to cry. I run to Javi and tell him I want to go home now.

The car ride home is quiet. I don't want to talk to Javi or tell him what happened. When we get home, I run inside past Mami and go into my room. Before I know it, Mami is in my room.

"Why are you crying, Mika? Is everything alright?" she asks.

"No. I'm sad," I reply.

She asks me what happened at school, and I tell her that Brooke won't play with me because she is mean. I also told her how I threw my friendship bracelet at her.

"It's okay, Mika," she tells me, "Tomorrow, Brooke will be nice again."

Mami leaves the room, but I know that things may never be the same with Brooke.

* * *

Today at school, Ms. Owens passes out sheets of paper and paintbrushes for art. I volunteer to help her pass out the paint and when I get to Brooke's table, I accidentally spill some paint on her. Brooke dips her paintbrush into the spilled paint and splatters it all over me. I get mad so I open a bottle of paint and pour it on her new shirt.

"Ahh! Mika look what you did! You made a huge mess, and now you have to clean it up!"

"It's not my fault."

"Yes, it is Mika. You started it."

Ms. Owens walks towards me and Brooke and pulls us apart.

"Girls, what is going on?"

Brooke starts blaming the whole thing on me. Ms. Owens turns towards me and tells me I am in trouble and have to go sit by myself facing the wall. When she tries to take me to go sit down, I start to scream and fall to the ground not letting her pick me up.

"Mika! Get up right now!" Ms. Owens yells at me, while Brooke is chuckling in the background.

I refuse and stay lying on the floor.

"That's it! I'm calling your mother!"

AVA

Well, the principal and Ms. Owens do not take the matter lightly. When I show up at the meeting, Mr. McAllen, the principal, has a very serious expression on his face. Ms. Owens is sitting beside him behind a very large mahogany desk.

"Good morning Ms. Owens," David kindly says to her. She nods in return.

"Hello Mr. McAllen, nice to see you," my husband tells the principal.

Both the principal and Mika's teacher stand up to shake our hands and greet us. We sit on the other side of the desk, and Ms. Owens begins blabbering on about Mika's, and I quote, "increasingly poor" behavior in the classroom. I immediately interject.

"I hate to interrupt, Ms. Owens, but I believe she only acted up yesterday in class simply because her *best friend* Brooke has been mean to her over the past two days."

"Ava, your daughter purposely threw paint on Brooke in the classroom during art. I don't see how Brooke could have provoked her to do such a thing," Ms. Owens says.

That got me angry, "Mika told me last night about the entire incident, and she told me that it was all an accident. She said Brooke threw paint on her in return because she had been mean to her. Brooke doesn't want to be her friend anymore because Mika is different and slower than all the other kids in the class."

Mr. McAllen sits there, listening intently and refuses to get involved. My husband finally brings him into the conversation. "So Mr. McAllen, with all due respect, why did you request our presence this morning?"

"Mr. and Mrs. Torres," he begins, "I called the two of you because I am becoming concerned with Mika being in this school. She is the only child with special needs in the school and—"

"She's been doing perfectly fine all these years, so why pull her out now? I don't know where I'd put her,

Mr. McAllen. Please allow her to stay at least for the remainder of the year!" I plead.

"Alright. But on one condition: Mika must not act up again in the class, and if I am called once more about her poor behavior, she will not be able to stay. I am terribly sorry."

"Thanks for your concern," David scoffs. I nudge him in the stomach. He lets out a small chuckle.

"All I'm trying to say is, Mika must improve her behavior," Ms. Owens states.

"I understand," I say, "I just would like to make it clear that her oldest best friend is leaving her, and I feel sorry for my daughter, and I understand why she would be 'acting up' in your classroom, Ms. Owens. She doesn't know any other way to deal with her emotions."

The principal's secretary walks into his office and reminds him that his next appointment is waiting outside.

"Thank you for coming, and I am sorry about Mika's loss of her friendship. I will make sure that Ms. Owens will have a word with Brooke about it," Mr. McAllen concludes.

My husband and I shake hands with McAllen and Ms. Owens again and walk over to the car. David drops me off at home and leaves for work. Olivia doesn't get out of school for another hour so I get into my car and go to Mika's gymnastics to pay for her upcoming session. When I arrive and write Mika's name down on the list of girls that will be taking the class, I see Brooke's name there as well. I pause to see if I should sign her up or not. Mika loves gymnastics and would be so disappointed if she finds out that I didn't put her in the class, so I decided to sign her up anyway. The first class is later today after school, and I know Mika will have to face Brooke, so I will have to let her know about it first.

Javi and Mika got home a little while after I got home with Olivia.

"Hi Mika! How was school?"

"Okay," she says, on her way to the playroom to watch T.V.

Javi walks past me in a hurry and goes to the bathroom. I didn't even get to say hi to him. I tell him to come back to the kitchen to ask him what he wants for dinner. He freaks out and I see him all beat up. He explains to me about getting into a fight with a football player, Frank, after school in the parking lot. They got in a huge fight because Frank was making fun of Mika.

"Well I'm glad you defended your little sister, but you need to get cleaned up. I've got to go to gymnastics. We'll talk later. Keep an eye on Olivia for me," I say.

I change Mika into her leotard for gymnastics and pull her hair back into a braid. "Time for gymnastics!" I say

"Yes gymnastics!" Mika replies with a smile across her face.

When we pull into TumbleTime gym, Grace, Brooke's mom, pulls in beside us. *Great.*

"C'mon, Mika. Time to get out of the car."

Mika squirms around a bit and shrieks as I unbuckle her seatbelt. "Mika," I beg, "Please. It's time for gymnastics. Let's get out of the car so we won't be late," I say, so I won't

47

have to deal with Brooke and Grace. I carry her out into the gym, and the gymnastics instructor greets Mika, who is very happy to see her. Behind us, enter Brooke and her mother. Brooke notices Mika and whispers in her mother's ear that she wants to go home. Grace does not let her leave and instead makes her go onto the mat. Mika sees Brooke and turns her back to her and starts to wail very loudly. The instructor immediately runs to her side and asks her what's wrong. Mika just screams Brooke's name and continues to cry. The instructor signals me to go and help her out. I run out to her and tell her to stop crying.

"Listen, Mika. It's all right. I know you're crying because Brooke's here, but you can just ignore her. I need you to be a big girl, okay?"

"Okay," Mika replies, wiping her tears.

The instructor mouths *thank you* as I leave Mika's side. I nod my head, and the instructor continues. She tells the girls that for the show which is next class, each girl will be paired up with a partner. Mika stands proud, excited to finally be in a show. The instructor goes around, pairing everybody up and ironically, Mika is paired with Brooke.

"No!" says Brooke, "I don't want to be with Mika! She's a baby!" "Ignore her," Mika mutters under her breath.

"Why don't you want to be with Mika, Brooke? She's your best friend?" asks the instructor.

"Not anymore! She's just a big baby," Brooke pouts.

"Well, I'm sorry Brooke. The two of you are partners and that's that." The instructor lets out a sigh and keeps on teaching the class routines.

JAVI

School goes by fast the next day, and while I'm walking back to my car talking with Ryan about the upcoming football game we have, I see Frank and the rest of his clan laughing and looking in my direction. I just ignore them and keep walking.

"Just ignore them Javi. They're only trying to bother you," Ryan says while he gets into his car before he leaves.

"Hey junior!"

I know he's talking about me, but I get into my car before he starts something. Frank suddenly steps in front of my car and says, "Oh, this kid thinks he can just ignore us, huh boys?" he says laughing.

Frank knocks on my window, so I roll it down.

"What do you want Frank?"

"Nothing, David here was just asking me, how long it would take your sister to spell her name. Then I said to him, 'I don't know. We'll all be dead by the time she does.'"

My face begins to fume up, and I can feel my muscles getting tense, and my fists closing together. Frank and all his friends just laugh in my face, acting as if nothing is wrong. I get out of the car and stand up right in front of Frank.

"Ohhh your gonna try to be the big guy huh? Gonna stand up for your retarded sister?"

I step closer into Frank, "What did you just call her?"

At this point I'm so close to Frank, our foreheads are touching, "I called her a retard." He pushes me away with his hand and turns around to walk to his car. I follow Frank and pull his shoulder to force him to turn around. POW! I punch Frank straight in the face. He immediately covers his nose that starts to drip with blood the instant I pull my fists back. I wipe the small amount of Frank's blood that is dripping down my knuckles on my jeans. Frank grins at me and begins to chuckle, like this is all a joke. I go to punch him one more time, but before I realize it, two of Frank's friends are holding my arms back not letting me go. Frank circles around me and starts to look up and down my body deciding where he will pound me first. He looks like a butcher trying to decide where to make the first cut into his tender meat. I try to escape from the grasp his two pals have on me, but they're too strong. Frank stops in front of me and gets so close I can see the outline my fist made on his face.

"Aw, how cute! Little Javi here is trying to defend his retard of a sister; well, too bad no one is here to see it."

I do the only thing I can do that doesn't include my hands. I spit on his face. Frank gets ticked off and goes for the first blow. He punches me on my right cheek. Next, he hits me in the stomach so hard that I fall to the ground.

"Leave him! He won't fight back. He's too scared," Frank starts to walk away with the rest of his gang.

I stand up with the little strength I have and run after Frank, push him to the floor, and start to beat the hell out of him. After pounding Frank for a sufficient amount, I get off him, look at his friends who have their jaws dropped, and walk back to my car.

On my way to pick Mika up from school, I replay the whole fight with Frank in mind. I keep wondering how he even knew about Mika and why he decided to bring her up now. I also go over the reason why I threw the first punch; Frank called my sister a retard. I hate that word, "retard". It's so degrading and offensive especially to those people with disabilities, like Mika. A lot of people aren't aware of the impact and offense that word has on people with physical or mental disabilities. Before I knew Mika had Down syndrome, I used to joke around and say, "You're a retard" and just refer to it as a harmless joke. I didn't know the true meaning of that word and how offended and mad people got when I or anyone else would say it. I know now that even jokingly calling someone a "retard" or referring to someone with a disability, retarded, is not only disrespectful but also hurtful.

I pull up to Mika's school and find her sitting down at a table by herself. I honk the horn. Mika runs up to my car and immediately a ginormous smile appears on her face.

"Javi!"

"Hey Mika! How was school?"

Mika looks down, "Ok."

I open the car door for her and tell her to get in so we can go home. On the way home, Mika tells me what she did in school but doesn't even mention Brooke or how she has been acting.

"So Mika, have you talked to Brooke?"

Mika doesn't bother to answer. She just shakes her head and asks me if she can play some music.

"Sure, what do you want to listen to?"

"'To The Left!'" she says with enthusiasm. It's actually called "Irreplaceable," but that's what she calls it.

"Mika I don't have that song, what about 'Dynamite'?"

"Yes!"

I put the song on and Mika starts to sing along to the words and dance to the beat. We get home right when the song ends, and Mika jumps out of the car and runs to the door. I get off the car and open the door for her; she runs inside to the playroom to watch T.V.

"Is that you Javi?"

"Yeah! It's me."

I try to avoid my mom so she won't see my face and ask how I got hurt. I go straight to the bathroom to wash my face and blood out. I look into the mirror and see a red mark on the side of my face, and a bruise already starting to form around the corner of my eye. I lift my shirt and can see the outline of Frank's fist perfectly in the middle of my stomach. I walk out of the bathroom and head to the kitchen so I can get an ice pack for my eye. Once I enter the kitchen, I see my mom unpacking some groceries. I turn around and start to walk to my room.

"Javi, wait. Come back. I need to ask you something."

Great she knows; she knows about the fight, and now I'll probably be grounded for life.

"Mami, it's not as bad as it looks," I say, walking into the kitchen. "Oh my God! Javi what happened? What did you do?"

"Wait. You didn't know? I thought—"

"No, I didn't know! I was going to ask you what you want for dinner tonight."

"Oh wow. I thought you knew about all this," I say pointing to my wrecked face.

"How did this happen?"

I sit down at the kitchen table and explain the whole fight to my mom word by word so she will understand why I did what I did.

"Javi, why didn't you just ignore them? They were just trying to get to you, and I guess they did," she says, placing an icepack on my face.

"Mami, they were making fun of Mika. They called her a 'retard'. What was I supposed to do?"

"Nothing. You shouldn't have done anything. You are supposed to be the bigger person."

I shake my head and look up to my mom, "Sometimes it's hard to be the bigger person, Mom. I can't always ignore everyone who makes fun of these poor kids with disabilities, and especially my own sister."

"Javi, I know its hard but—" I cut off my mom before she can say anything else, "It's really hard; it's hard having a sister that people make fun of and knowing that one day you will have to stand up for her. But it's worth it Mami, beating Frank up; he acted as if it was fine to just make fun of Mika to my face. It wasn't."

"I know it's not ok, but you can get in trouble for this Javi. You shouldn't have even touched Frank; you should have just left him."

"But I didn't and don't regret it Mom. He deserved it. How does Frank even know about Mika?"

"He has a little brother in her class, and I guess that's how he found out about Mika and how she acted up."

"Oh, I guess."

My mom kisses me on the forehead and tells me I'm not in trouble. She leaves to get Mika cleaned up for dinner. I get up from the table and walk back to my room to rest for a bit. I lie down on my bed and try to clear my head and erase the fight I had with Frank. But I can't. I needed to stand up for Mika, even if it meant getting hurt.

MIKA

"Good morning class!" Ms. Owens says, "Today, the first thing we will be learning about is multiplication. Now pick a partner, and I will hand out some sheets with different problems on them. You will solve these problems with your partner."

I immediately look at Brooke, but she is already sitting next to Haley, talking and giggling. I stay in my seat and put my head down, hoping Ms. Owens doesn't notice me. I feel someone tap my shoulder, and I turn to see Ms. Owens standing next to Freddie, the new boy.

"Mika, why don't you pair up with Freddie? He doesn't have a partner either."

"No!"

Ms. Owens looks at Freddie and tells him to sit down anyway. I don't talk to Freddie. I put my head down again and stay quiet. Freddie doesn't bother asking me any questions; he goes along and does all the problems by himself.

Ring! Ring! Ring! Everyone turns to the phone that is hanging on the wall by Ms. Owens's desk.

"Hello? . . . . Yes of course . . . . I will be right down."

Ms. Owens hangs up and walks back to her desk and picks up a stack of papers that are laying there.

"Class, I have to go to a meeting now, so Mrs. Harrison will be teaching you until I return."

Mrs. Harrison doesn't really pay attention to what we are doing, so everyone is goofing around and not doing work. When Ms. Owens returns, nobody had done their worksheets.

"Alright class, since all of you decided to play around while I was gone, you have to do these worksheets for homework."

"Aw man," everyone mumbles under their breath. I can't wait until school's over.

I walk out to the front of the school and sit down at an empty table. I see Brooke walk away with Haley and her new friends. She doesn't even say hi to me or look my way. I hear a car horn honk and look up to find Javi's car. I'm thrilled to see Javi; I just want to be with someone who actually likes me right now.

"Javi!" I say with enthusiasm.

Javi asks me how school was, and I tell him everything we did, but I left out the part of Brooke not talking to me. He tries to get me to mention Brooke, but instead I shake my head and ask if I can listen to music.

"Sure, what do you want to listen to?" Javi asks.

All I can think of is my favorite song, "'To The Left!'"

Javi tells me that he doesn't have the song, so instead he puts on "Dynamite."

As soon as the song starts playing, I begin to sing along and dance to the beat of the music. The song ends right when Javi pulls up at home. I run out of the car and straight into the playroom to watch T.V. Before I can go into the playroom, Mami stops me.

"Hi Mika. How was school?" she asks.

"Okay."

I go into the playroom and turn on the T.V to escape. Mami comes into the room and tells me I have to get ready for gymnastics. I love gymnastics, it's so fun, and I think I'm good at it too. Mami puts on my leotard for gymnastics and braids my hair right before we leave.

The car ride to the gymnastics place was fun; Mami and me listened to music and laughed. But when Mami parked, I saw Brooke and her mom. I don't want to go to gymnastics anymore.

"C'mon, Mika. Time to get out of the car."

I don't want to get out so I begin to twist and squirm not letting my mom grab me.

"Mika, please." She begs me to get out. I finally let Mami carry me out of the car to go into the building. When I get into gymnastics, I run to the mat where Annie, the instructor, is waiting. Brooke walks in after me and sits next to me but turns her back so she won't have to talk to me. I get so mad when Brooke turns away, so I just start to scream. Annie asks me what's wrong, but I ignore her and keep screaming. My mom suddenly appears at my side and tells me to be a big girl and stop screaming. I finally stop and wipe the few tears from my face.

Once class begins, Annie tells us that we have a show next class, and we will do it with a partner. I can see Brooke mutter under her breath, praying not to be paired up with me. Coincidentally, guess who my partner is?

"No!" Brooke says staring me down, "I don't want to be with Mika! She's a baby!"

I want to tell Brooke that I'm not too happy about this either, but at least I'm not complaining but nothing comes out. I can see Brooke telling Annie that she doesn't like me anymore, and we are not friends. But Annie still makes her stay as my partner and tells her she won't change it. I just think to myself, this next week will be a long one filled with screaming, fighting, and maybe even crying.

* * *

I invited Brooke over after school today to work on our gymnastics routine. Well, of course, I didn't invite her; she would've said no to me right away. Mami called her mom yesterday instead. They were on the phone for a long time. During lunch, I remind Brooke that she's going home with me in front of all her friends. I don't think Brooke is very happy about that. She looks embarrassed, even. She nods her head and turns back around to take a bite of her string cheese, our—I mean *my*—favorite snack.

Javi picks us up, and I sing and dance to my favorite songs like always. Brooke doesn't talk the whole car ride home, but I'm used to her not talking now, I guess. When we get home, Mami has *pollitos* and *papitas* from McDonalds in the kitchen. That made me happy.

"Hi everybody!" Mami says and kisses me and Javi on the cheek. "Nice to see you, Brooke," she says.

After eating our food, Mami tells us to go outside to the backyard so we can practice. Brooke isn't so good at gymnastics. I'm way more flexible than she is. My split goes all the way to the floor! Hers doesn't. I tell Mami that, and she says not to worry. Brooke won't be doing any splits in the routine. *Whew.*

"Brooke," I tell her, "it's okay. You aren't doing any splits in the routine!"

She lets out a small giggle. "Thanks," she says. Wow, did Brooke just laugh? I think I heard a laugh! I smile at her. She grins back.

AVA

Mika's gymnastics show is in two days, and Mika and Brooke haven't practiced anything. I feel sorry for Mika because she was partnered up with her new enemy Brooke. Well, I wouldn't say that Brooke is *Mika's* enemy; it's the other way around. Mika is *Brooke's* enemy. So I'm actually sort of glad that the two are partnered up because maybe this will resolve their issues. I know deep down that Brooke still cares a lot about Mika. I think she abandoned her because her new friends aren't quite—how should I put this—fond of Mika.

Anyway, I decide to call Grace, Brooke's mother, so the girls can meet up tomorrow after school to learn the routine.

"Hello?"

"Hi, Grace. It's me, Ava," I say dryly.

"Oh," Grace says, surprised.

"I'm calling so we can get the girls together tomorrow afternoon for the gymnastics routine.

The show is on Saturday, and they have nothing done. I think they should at least attempt to put something together."

"I'm not too sure if Brooke is up for that," she tells me.

"Well, you'll never know until you try," I say, sounding childish. But I know it's just what'll get Grace to send Brooke home with Mika tomorrow.

"I'm afraid Brooke has already made plans with Haley tomorrow after school."

"She can reschedule, I'm sure," I assume.

No reply.

"Listen, Grace. Our daughters must complete this routine by Saturday's show whether they—or we—like it or not. Brooke needs to cooperate with Mika this last time, at least. Your daughter's new so-called 'friends' who make her stay away from her old *true* friend will not be attending this show, so I don't understand why Brooke is still acting like Mika is no longer her friend," I demand.

"Alright," Grace answers, "I'll let Brooke know that she will be leaving home with Mika tomorrow instead of Haley. Call me tomorrow when they're done," she concludes sternly.

"Thank you, Grace," I respond as politely as possible. "See you tomorrow, then."

"See you tomorrow," she clicks off the phone.

That conversation was a bit uncomfortable. Grace and I never speak to each other like we just did. I guess we have nothing in common when our daughters don't either. It's funny the way things work sometimes.

*   *   *

It's Friday morning, and Olivia and Mika are all set for school.

"No school tomorrow!" Mika shouts.

"That's right, Mika! No school tomorrow!" I hear Olivia shout in return, as she waits by the front door.

"C'mon girls, go get into the car. It's unlocked. I've got to check on Javi."

Sure enough, right when I say so, he walks out of his room. Mika runs to him and hugs him. I warn him to hurry up, or else he'll be late, and then I'm off to drop of my daughters.

Later in the day after picking up Olivia from school, I pass by McDonald's and buy some chicken nuggets and fries for the girls. I know this'll make Mika happy when she walks through the door. Hopefully, Brooke will like the snack as well. When the two do get home with Javi, I say hello to each of them, and Javi goes straight to his room, as usual. I let the girls eat their snack as they do so silently.

"How was school, girls?" I ask to break the silence.

"Good," Mika replies. "Awesome," I say, "Well, girls, are you finished? When you are done, get all cleaned up and meet me outside in the back so we can get to work!"

Brooke nods her head as she takes her last bite. I go to the backyard and slide the glass door closed. I watch Mika and Brooke as they throw away their trash. I see

Mika collect all her things and walk enthusiastically to the trashcan, and when she tosses her food away, she chuckles, all proud of herself. She always knows how to make me smile. I notice that Brooke sees that Mika is finished clearing the table, and I see that Brooke grabs her hand and takes her outside. Mika smiles her brightest smile and follows Brooke with excitement.

"Okay, girls. Let's get started!" I play the music and go along teaching the girls the dance moves for the routine. Brooke seems bored and doesn't make eye contact with Mika, even though I watch as Mika stares at her best friend with a smile on her face.

"Mami, come!" Mika shouts to me.

"Be right there," I pause the music and head on over to Mika's side.

"Mami, Brooke can't do a split!" she whispers in my ear. I tell her not to worry because Brooke won't be doing any splits in the routine, and Mika tells her right away. Brooke thanks Mika and laughs for the first time in what seems like forever. Mika grins in return.

With the routine finally completed, I call Grace and let her know that it's time to pick up Brooke. When Grace does arrive, she doesn't get out of her car. Instead, she just calls the house and tells Brooke that she's waiting for her outside. Brooke hangs up and waves goodbye to us and runs out the door. I turn to Mika, expecting her to be sad for not being able to actually say goodbye to her friend, but instead, I find her glistening and jumping up and down, glad that she was finally able to hang out with her best friend.

* * *

"Everybody! Time to get in the car! We don't want our little gymnastics star to be late for her recital!"

I look at Mika who is standing by my side, and I see how beautiful she looks in her bright pink leotard full of sparkles and stars. Her hair is pulled back in a tight bun with hairspray. We added a cute pink scrunchy to go around the bun. Mika told me she was so excited to do the gymnastics show, and she thinks Brooke is excited too. The rest of the family gathers on the front porch, and David locks the door behind him. We get into the car, and Mika doesn't stop babbling on about how pretty she looks and how great everything will turn out to be. She doesn't seem to be worried at all about Brooke. She is very confident that nothing will go wrong. I wish I could be as optimistic as she, but sadly, I'm not. I pray in the car that Brooke will cooperate with Mika and that after the show, things will go back to the way they were. I also hope to make amends with Grace. I know Mika will do wonderfully and that she will make me proud no matter what. Every mom on the planet thinks the same thing. I just know that it'll all turn out okay.

When we finally get to TumbleTime Gym, Brooke is already inside, adding some finishing touches to the little makeup Grace applied to her face.

"Hi Brooke! Hi Brooke!" Mika yells. I think she believes she and Brooke are back to normal. That must explain why she's been so happy.

"Hey, Mika," Brooke responds with little emotion.

"Hi, Grace," I say, following Mika's path.

"Hello, Ava. Nice to see you. How are you?" Grace smiles.

"Fine, thank you. I'm just hoping our girls will do great!" I say with enthusiasm.

"We will," I hear Brooke say.

Annie, the instructor, walks over to us and tells us that the show will be starting soon. Grace and I take a seat with the rest of the crowd as Annie takes the girls to the back.

"I think our girls will do just fine," says Grace.

I don't notice until now that my legs were shaking. Grace must've noticed though. "What? Oh yeah, sure. They'll be okay," I hope.

"Ava, I know the girls will work it out. Brooke can't stay away from Mika forever. She loves your daughter. She always talks about her at home. She just got embarrassed, I guess. And it must be hard now that they're older. Mika's just slower than she is, and Brooke is starting to realize that. I've talked to her about it and that's exactly what she told me. I know you understand. But when Brooke realizes that even though Mika's different, they're still best friends."

"Thanks, Grace. I understand," I say. That helped me a lot. Now Grace and I are back to normal again, which makes me feel better.

"Ladies and gentlemen! Welcome to the TumbleTime gymnastics recital!" Annie recites, as she comes onto the mat with a microphone in hand. There are only about twenty people in the audience, because there's only about eight kids in the class, so Annie doesn't really need a microphone, but I think it is a nice touch. Christina and Maggie take the mat first, probably because they are the oldest. Their routine is great, full of flips and jumps. Mika and Brooke go last, and my anticipation builds as the other two groups behind Christina and Maggie perform.

Annie finally announces that it is Mika and Brooke's turn to go, and everyone claps for them as they walk onto the mat. Mika finds me in the audience and waves at me and yells "hi", and everybody laughs. I place my finger over my lips and wave back to her, a tear in my eye. Brooke holds onto Mika, and they smile at each other. I hear the music begin, and Mika lets out an excited roar. I close my eyes and thank God for my precious family and for my angel. I've got a great life, and I've got Mika. I feel more tears rush down my cheeks, and I open my eyes again. Then, it hits me. I know that Mika and Brooke are best friends once more.

Turns out, everything's going to be okay after all.

JAVI

Beeeep! Beeeep! My hand smacks the alarm clock, and I lay in bed for an extra five minutes before I get up for school. I hear Mika running up and down the hallway shouting for Olivia and I to wake up, like she does every morning. I really don't feel like going to school today; Frank is going to be highly annoying, and I don't want to even talk to him.

"Javi, c'mon, wake up. It's already 7:25. You're going to be late," Mami says.

I pull the covers over my head and turn away from the light that is shining in from the window.

"A couple more minutes."

"Fine, but it won't be my fault when you're sitting in detention after school."

My mom closes the door, and I stay lying in bed as if the conversation never happened. I usually would care about late detention, but at this point, with what happened with

Frank and all, I don't even want to show up at school. After contemplating whether I should go to school or not, I made my decision to go. I get out of bed and get dressed, before my mom comes in again raging with anger. Its already 7:30 by the time I get out of my room, and my mom is heading out of the door with Mika and Olivia.

"Well, look who decided to get out of bed," my mom says sarcastically.

"Sorry, I'm just so tired today," I say, rubbing my eyes.

Mika runs up to me and gives me a much-needed hug.

"Good morning, Javi!"

I bend down to kiss Mika on the cheek and whisper in her ear, "I love you."

"Love you, too."

Mika runs back to Mami and gets in the car for school. I wave goodbye as the car backs out of the driveway. I realize its past 7:30, and I actually don't want to go to detention. I chug down the rest of the orange juice that is in the carton, and finish the rest of Olivia's toast that she left on the table. I get to school a second before the front door closes. I see Ryan before I get into first period, and he tells me Frank wasn't in homeroom. I'm in shock; did I force Frank to stay home? Whatever the reason, at least I don't have to put up with his obnoxious comments and sarcasm today. When I walk into the cafeteria for lunch, all eyes are on me. I sit down next to Ryan cautiously.

"Why is everyone staring?"

"They all know about what went down between you and Frank. They know you socked him," Ryan says in a low tone.

I turn away from the people staring and start eating. The stares disappear when Frank walks in the cafeteria. Ryan nudges my elbow, "Javi." I turn around to find Frank staring down at me with a straight face. I am taken away by the damage I did to his face, a purple and blue bruise surrounds his left eye. There is a scar running down the right side of his face and small scrapes on the tip of his nose.

"Frank, how's your face?"

Frank laughs and pulls my shirt causing me to stand up, "Look, I heard you were telling everyone how you 'pounded me' yesterday."

"What are you talking about? I never told anyone that," I turn around and look down at Ryan who is trying to avoid my eye contact.

"Please, you must have been ecstatic when you got one punch in."

I look back at Frank, "One punch? I beat you to the ground Frank."

The entire cafeteria starts laughing and are in shock. Frank is speechless; he just stands there staring at me.

"I wouldn't have touched you if you didn't bring my sister into it."

Frank still doesn't say a word; I sit back down next to Ryan forgetting about Frank.

"I wouldn't have said anything to you if your sister wasn't, you know, retarded," he says laughing. I drop my fork and clench on to the table. Ryan tells me not to say anything, not to start something. I let go of the table and calm down. I don't bother to turn around. That's just what he wants. After a while of being silent, Frank walks out of the cafeteria with his gang following shortly behind. It was hard not to say anything to Frank. This time I was the bigger person. After the whole charade with Frank, everyone goes back to minding their own business.

"Nice job man, keeping your cool and all," Ryan says on the way back to class.

After school, I drive to go pick Mika up, and I remember that Brooke is coming home with us too. I pull up to Mika's school and see Mika and an unhappy Brooke sitting next to her. Mika sees my car and runs inside with Brooke trudging behind. Once both girls are in the car, I blast Mika's songs and put all the windows down. Brooke doesn't move a muscle.

"Hey, Brooke!" I say with a fake smile.

"Hi, Javi," she says with a dead voice.

Mika is dancing and singing to the music while Brooke looks out the window; I'm sure wishing to be somewhere else. When I pull up to the house, Brooke opens the door and gets out of the car, Mika following behind her. Mika runs past Brooke inside the house; Brooke slowly walks inside. I get into the house and find Mami with a bag of *pollitos* and *papitas*.

"Hi Javi!"

"Hey!" I say with a mouth full of French fries.

"Javi! Those are for the girls."

"Sorry, but you know they are my weakness," I say filling my hand with more fries. As I am walking out of the kitchen, Mika and Brooke are running in to eat the fries and chicken nuggets. I go into my room and lay down in bed. My mom walks in shortly after reminding me not to make plans tomorrow afternoon because Mika has her recital. I nod my head and lay back down.

I start to think about Mika and how she has affected my own life. By Mika having Down syndrome, I can see how hard it is for her to do certain things. I can see what makes her sad, mad, and happy. Mika is a caring loving person; she doesn't see anyone as being a different color or race; she views everyone the same. Mika has taught me to love equally and treat everyone the same in every way. Sometimes I can see my parents struggling with Mika. I can see how hard it is for them. But I remind them that Mika was sent to us for a reason. She is our angel, and God has a special plan for her. The way Mika has impacted my life is indescribable. She has and always will be the reason why I am who I am now and will grow to be.

MIKA

After I eat *pollo empanizado* for dinner, Mami tells me
its time for bed. I run to my room actually excited for the
next day. Tomorrow is the gymnastics recital, and I think
Brooke and me are friends again.

"Alright Mika, time to go to sleep," Mami says.

I jump in my bed and pull my cover up from under
me. Mami and I pray before she leaves to go clean up the
kitchen. As soon as we are done praying, I give Mami a
kiss on the cheek and a big hug. When she turns off the
lights and closes the door, I close my eyes trying to make
myself go to sleep faster. Nothing I do makes me sleepy,
because I'm too excited for the show. I finally fall asleep
and start to dream.

In my dream, I am in the same place I was before. But
now it's not as cold or dark, and I'm not scared or lonely. I
look up and see the bright sun shining down on me again.
The sun makes me feel good; I am happy. I finally found

the sun. Standing right under the sun is Brooke, and she's smiling. I run up to Brooke, and she greets me with open arms. We hug each other, and I am so happy we are friends again. I wake up really early the next morning and run to wake Mami and Papi up.

"Wake up! Wake up!" I say while jumping on Mami and Papi's bed.

"Hey big girl, good morning!" Papi says, sitting up.

"Good morning sweetie!" Mami says, kissing my forehead. She looks at the clock and then back at me and says, "Mika, what are you doing here so early in the morning? It's barely five in the morning."

"Show today," I say.

"That's right, Mika! Today is your gymnastics show. That must explain why you're up so early: you're too excited to get any sleep. Come here," Papi tells me and pats a spot next to him on the bed.

I jump onto the bed and snuggle up next to him, and I nod my head in response to his explanation as to why I'm awake. Minutes later, Papi and Mami are sleeping again, so I just look up at the ceiling until they wake up again. When they do wake up, I tell Papi to make me my favorite breakfast: pancakes! (With a side of my baby cereal. Sadly, I can't avoid that). Mami walks over tiredly to Olivia's room to wake her up. Then, she goes to Javi's room to do the same. I run over to the kitchen with Papi to help with breakfast.

After we eat, Mami lets me watch some T.V. before I have to get ready for the show. I click on the T.V and decide to watch Ariel again. I love that movie. Me and Brooke always used to watch Ariel. We would sing along to all the songs. When Ariel is over, I go to my room to get ready for the show.

"Mika, let's go. It's show time!" Mami says excitingly.

"Getting ready!" I shout.

Mami helps me finish getting ready, and puts on my make up while I rehearse my part in my head.

"Mami, me and Brooke are going to be great!"

Mami looks at me through the mirror and smiles, "I know you will be."

When I'm done getting ready, we all get into the car and drive to the gymnastics place. On the way there, I think about the routine and how good Brooke and me are going to do. I can see Mami is scared we won't be good, but I'll make sure we do our best today. We get to the gymnastics place an hour before the show starts. Papi, Javi, and Olivia go get something to eat before the show starts, and Mami comes backstage with me. When we get there, we see Brooke's mom putting some makeup on Brooke.

"Hi Brooke!" I say with excitement.

Brooke waves back at me, "Hey Mika!"

Mami and Brooke's mom leave from backstage and go to sit down. I walk over to Brooke who is sitting down playing with her DS and sit next to her.

"Mika, I'm glad you are my partner for the routine. You make the routine special, and besides, if it weren't for you, nobody would cheer the loudest when we go on stage and we wouldn't be the last act!" Brooke tells me and I laugh. "Anyway, I'm really sorry about what's been going on this past week. I shouldn't have been so rude to you. Do you forgive me?"

"Yes," I say as I give her a big hug, "It's okay, Brooke."

I notice it's our turn to go on. I grab Brooke's hand, and we run to the side of the mat. Brooke takes her spot across from me and smiles before the music starts. Once "Lollipop" begins, we start our routine. I see Mami in the audience and scream out "Hi!" to her. Me and Brooke are doing so good. Everyone is clapping and giggling at everything we do. When we finish our routine, everyone stands up and claps before we go backstage. As I walk off, Brooke takes me by the hand and returns me to the center of the mat. She raises our hands, and we take a bow. The crowd goes wild! She then hugs me and whispers to me, "Best friends?" I answer, "Best friends."

AUTHORS' NOTE

Mika is a girl who was born with a disability called Down syndrome. Down syndrome is also known as Trisomy 21, and it is a chromosomal defect where the child is born with an extra forty-seven chromosomes instead of the usual forty-six. Children who are born with Down syndrome have unique physical features. They have small ears, flat faces, walnut-shaped eyes, and a projecting tongue. Individuals who are diagnosed with Down syndrome tend to grow at a slower rate than the average person, and they have trouble learning, usually having to go to different kinds of therapies in order to keep up. Those who have this disability usually have other medical conditions including having trouble hearing, seeing, speaking, and heart defects.

Although Down syndrome is a disability, it is a true blessing to have a person with Down syndrome in your life. That one person changes the way you view the world and everyone around you; they open your heart and help you become a better person in every way.

For more information on Down syndrome visit <u>www. DSAOM.org</u>

ACKNOWLEDGEMENTS

First off, we would like to thank our parents for pushing us to complete this book and for always believing in us. You are always there for us and never gave up hope. Thanks for all your support.

A special thanks to our entire family, you guys have been the greatest!

We would also like to thank our eighth grade English teacher, Mrs. Febo who helped us through the writing process of this book. Without you none of this would have been possible. Thank you so much.

We thank God for blessing us with all that we have in our lives, and the people we have encountered along the way.

Last, but certainly not least we thank the girl who inspired us to write this book, my sister and my cousin, Dani. She inspires us everyday and teaches us the beauty in life. Our main character Mika is based on Dani and her actions. Without her this book would have never come to life. She may not realize it, but we are learning from her everyday and she will always be our little angel. We love you and thanks!

CPSIA information can be obtained at www.ICGtesting.com
Printed in the USA
LVOW11*1457290915

456188LV00005B/24/P